SON OF A BIRD
A MEMOIR IN PROSE POEMS

Also by Nin Andrews

The Last Orgasm

Miss August

Our Lady of the Orgasms

Why God Is a Woman

The Secret Life of Mannequins

Southern Comfort

Dear Professor, Do You Live in a Vacuum

Sleeping with Houdini

Midlife Crisis with Dick and Jane

Any Kind of Excuse

Someone Wants to Steal My Name (editor)

The Book of Orgasms and Other Tales

Why They Grow Wings

Spontaneous Breasts

The Book of Orgasms

Son of a Bird confirms indisputably that Nin Andrews is the greatest living technician of the prose poem in America. Andrews ranks with Edson, Simic, Benedikt, and Tate, as a virtuoso in the form that calls all poetic form into question. *Son of a Bird* is a memoir unwinding in vibrant lyric shards, bravely exploring the racial dynamics, the sexual politics, and the disappointments and consolations of family life below the Mason-Dixon line. By turns staunchly bucolic, achingly painful, riotously funny, and ruinously alive, the world Andrews arrays around us in this book vibrates with curses and wishes, birdsong and shadow, sunlight and the black smoke of burning alfalfa fields caused by a cricket's fiddling. Andrews speaks across time to her past self, to her gay father, to her autistic mother, and to the mid-twentieth century South—and in speaking thus, she enjoins her readers to scan the fields of their own pasts, hunting for "memories like scared mice scampering through the grass." Like that other famous Southern genius, Andrews knows the past is never truly past, it just keeps piping away in the nest outside your living room. *Son of a Bird* reminds us to open all the windows, listen, and hum along.

—Dante Di Stefano,
Midwhistle

Memoirs by their very nature must rely on self-consciousness and introspection, but when that self-consciousness ends up being nothing more than psychic bloodletting, we end up with an author who often ignores both language and her reader. Nin Andrews avoids these pitfalls in her hybrid gem of a book, *Son of a Bird*. By juxtaposing short prose sections that themselves straddle the precarious boundaries between the fragment, the prose poem, and many other genres, she invites us to piece together the coming-of-age story of a Southern girl struggling with emotional and physical setbacks in a world dvoid of stable adults to guide her. The beautiful writing here is lyrical, tragic, yet also oftentimes comic—all of these forces allowing her to create an authentic character we will never forget. Every time I reread this book, I still marvel at the poetry and wisdom in it.

—Peter Johnson,
While the Undertaker Sleeps: Collected and New Prose Poems

In *Son of a Bird*, Nin Andrews presents a deeply moving ode to her childhood, painted against the backdrop of a Virginia farm. Through a series of evocative prose poems, we learn of her story—Andrews writes, *Once upon a time, there was a girl who didn't want to be born. She was the last daughter of a gay man and an autistic woman.* This is a childhood filled with poignancy and peculiarities from a pet bull named Melvin, a paper doll named Galaxy, a cross-eyed child who sees Death, and a Barbie graveyard with little cardboard caskets. Throughout it all, Andrews is a gifted storyteller who is able to confront heavy topics with a gentle touch and always with the beauty of a poet—*She bragged that we were farm children, raised by the animals, the wind, the stars, the rain.* Andrews also explores mental illness and suicidal ideation with honesty and insight during a period when these topics were hidden in secrecy and widely misunderstood. *Son of a Bird* is not just a story of overcoming physical and mental challenges; it's a testament to survival and a journey of finding one's place within a family and the larger world. And with Andrews weaving a narrative so captivating and vivid, it's nearly impossible to put the book down—this is a book so rich with story, it reminds me how thankful I am that there's a Nin Andrews in the world, writing the poems like no other can write—how lucky we are for her work.

—Kelli Russell Agodon,
Dialogues with Rising Tides

With equal parts rigor and vulnerability, *Son of a Bird*, a memoir in prose poems, lays bare the psychic and mythic reverberations of a deeply troubled childhood. Birthed at a time her mother was already "done in," Nin Andrews bravely recounts a life born out of complex family histories, exploring in page after page of lyrical vignettes issues of loss and wonder, privilege and peril, brushes with death alongside pulses of beauty. What emerges is a self and family portrait characterized by disconnect and addiction, neglect and dysfunction. What emerges for the poet-memoirist is a sense of fellowship with nature deep enough to save her—birds and cows, butterflies and grasshoppers "clinging to her legs with their Velcro claws." With courageous intensity, Andrews lifts this phenomenal book out of her chest and gifts it to us, her rapt and grateful readers.

—Diane Raptosh,
I Eric America

SON OF A BIRD
A MEMOIR IN PROSE POEMS

By Nin Andrews

Etruscan Press

Etruscan Press
Wilkes University
84 West South Street
Wilkes-Barre, PA 18766
(570) 408-4546

Wilkes
University

www.etruscanpress.org

Published 2025 by Etruscan Press
Printed in the United States of America
Cover design by Jess Morandi
Interior design and typesetting by Joseph Schwartz
The text of this book is set in Whitman.

First Edition

17 18 19 20 5 4 3 2 1

Library of Congress Cataloging–in–Publication Data

Names: Andrews, Nin, author.
Title: Son of a bird / by Nin Andrews.
Description: Wilkes Barre, PA : Etruscan Press, 2025. | Summary: "Son of a Bird is a provocative encounter of girlhood, farm life and longing, hauntings and huntings, the self's instability, and the place where desire and the strange/unusual/unconventional/ meet. Son of a Bird is a memoir in the tradition of Dorothy Allison and Flannery O'Connor. Surrounded by farm hands and wild, lush isolation, due to constant eye surgeries, the youngest of six children, Nin Andrews observes the world at a tilt. In this collection of prose poems, hunted by death and the brutalities of farm life, Andrews begins to connect the small black dots of her upbringing--her father's relationships with men, her mother's autism, and the burdens of childhood awakenings--ultimately cracking through the shadows that haunt her."-- Provided by publisher.
Identifiers: LCCN 2024037123 | ISBN 9798988198598 (paperback)
Subjects: LCGFT: Prose poems.
Classification: LCC PS3551.N444 S66 2025 | DDC 811/.54--dc23/eng/20241209
LC record available at https://lccn.loc.gov/2024037123

Please turn to the back of this book for a list of the sustaining funders of Etruscan Press.

In writing *Son of a Bird*, I told one story of my childhood, but it is only one of many stories, or one collection of memories. In any memoir, there is so much one must leave out. And of course, all memory is flawed. As the youngest of six children, I have learned that each of my siblings tells a different version of our childhood.

Growing up in a large family on a farm with horses, cows, chickens, pigs, and many caretakers was like growing up in a beehive—there was so much happening all at once, so many people coming and going. As a consequence, I created some composite characters. I have changed the names of certain individuals out of respect for their privacy.

Oh dream, why do you do me this way?
Again, with the digging, again with the digging up.
Once more with the shovel.
Once more, the shovels full of dirt.
The vault lid. The prying. The damp boards.

~Diane Seuss

In the midst of winter, I found there was, within me,
an invincible summer.

~Albert Camus

For my sister, Sal, who saved my life.

Table of Contents

Acknowledgements

Many thanks to the editors of the following literary journals in which some of the poems originally appeared, some in earlier versions: *Agni, The Best American Poetry Blog, DMQ, Green Mountain Review, Hole in the Head Review, The Mackinaw, a journal of prose poetry, Ploughshares, Plume.* Also, many thanks to the editors of the anthology, *I Wanna Be Loved by You, Poems on Marilyn Monroe.* And to the kind and generous editors at Etruscan Press: Philip Brady, Amanda Rabaduex, and Pamela Turchin.

I am eternally grateful to my husband, Jim, my son, Jimmy, my daughter, Suzanne, and my many poet-friends including Denise Duhamel, Kathleen McGookey, Peter Johnson, Rick Bursky, Jeff Friedman, Stephanie Strickland, Jessica Jacobs, and Nancy Mitchell. Without their encouragement, I would never have been able to write this book.

Acknowledgments

Dear Past Self

When I visited my childhood home last week,
I could see you in the windows of our stone farmhouse
with your pink glasses and tiny eyes . . .
No, you weren't ever that small, but that's how I see you
now, as small as Thumbelina, and our house too, and the barns
where the horses and chickens slept, where the kittens
and foals were born each spring. Once, when the horses kicked
their stalls and whinnied in the night, you ran barefoot in the dark,
flashlight in hand, to check on them, and back in bed, unable to sleep
and out of breath, you wrote, *Dear Future Me* in script, imagining
me now. That was the night Dad's horse, Ella, died. We phoned
the vet, but by the time he arrived, Ella was dead. You tried
to think of other things, like how you wanted to grow up and be
a horse, or the fastest runner on earth, or the best high jumper.
That's what you wished for on every birthday, star,
and on every point of pie which you saved to eat last
because otherwise your wish wouldn't come true—at least according
to your dad. You practiced eating grass, whinnying and trotting,
cantering and galloping, before jumping all the horse jumps
one by one. Sometimes you fell and skinned your knees
or banged your head, but you kept practicing until your legs ached,
and you were soaked with sweat. But still you couldn't sleep.
Dear Future Me, you wrote in entry after entry. *Please come back.*
Don't forget. Write about me. About the horse I am. Or almost am.
Only make me prettier. And fast. Back then you didn't love you very much
and hoped I'd make you better after the fact. Which is strange,
I think, for a child. Strange also to be an insomniac, already
staring out the window at the dark, afraid of sickness and death
and old age, already picturing yourself as an old woman looking back
or down, like an owl swooping over the fields of the past,
memories like scared mice scampering through the grass.

The Book in My Chest

It started when I was in college after I left the family farm, this habit I have of keeping a book inside my chest—an illustrated text, complete with drawings, photos, fantasies, memories, poems, old letters, but no one has ever read it. (I suspect everyone has one, that they're as common as prayer books left in churches with black moleskin covers.) In dreams I find myself turning the pages, folding the corners, underlining passages. I can still see it in the mirror when I wake up, but of course all the words are backwards.

Mornings, I wash my face, put on my glasses, and lean in, squinting to take a closer look at my pages before the words drift away in schools of tiny black fish. I try to translate them as if they're a foreign language, but some have no meaning. I don't even know where the book begins. If I go back too far, the pages disintegrate. Or turn into winged insects—termites, bees, moths. What is the price of letting them disappear? And what of the drawings? The oceans my father water-colored so many times, each one tossed aside, curling up on the porch like an abandoned thought. (A perfectionist, nothing was ever good enough for my father.) My mother's cows graze on the rolling hillside. On the lawn my sisters hold hands in a game of Red Rover Red Rover. They look so drippy and faint as if the sky were crying overhead. "I dare you to come over," one calls and sticks out her tongue. The colors brighten as they tighten their grip on one another's wrists. Overhead, Death circles, sweeping the sky with his wings.

Stuck in the early pages of the book is an old photograph. The farm where I grew up is in the background, my bald father with browline glasses and a tweed trilby hat and my mother with her hair permed tight as a poodle's are in the middle ground. In the foreground are my four sisters and Miss Mary, the nanny. Miss Mary is holding me, a screaming, cross-eyed towheaded baby, in her large black arms. If you look closely, you can see a halo above her head. Or is it just a fingerprint from all the times I touched her face? My brother is absent. I no longer know him. He took himself out of the picture long ago. "Why?" you might ask. I don't have to tell you.

In a later chapter, I stand at the edge of a stone ledge. A tiny ledge, a dizzying view. Each minute I stand there, the ledge shrinks. "What the hell are you doing up there?" my father shouts. He says he thought he raised me with common sense. "The ground is covered with pine needles," my mother shrugs, certain I will have a soft landing no matter how far I fall. (My mother is immune to worry.) "You're just trying to get attention," one sister calls out as the ledge crumbles and the air opens around me. *What a relief!* To feel just air, to hear the wind in my ears, no advice, no shame holding me in place. *I could get used to this,* I think as my life flashes by, a blaze of color and speed.

In page after page, I am in hospitals: a skinny, freckled girl, stretched out in a bed, fast asleep. The doctor enters my room, inserts a tube into my nose and throat. "This won't hurt," he whispers. He says he will drain the signs. Maybe he meant sinuses. I am young enough to play with paper dolls. I know this because I pull a paper doll from my pocket and introduce her to the doctor. "Her name is Galaxy," I say. "She's scared. I have another doll called White Lightning, but she's invisible. And another one called Gazelle." Back then I talked to the doctor and the nurses, even in my sleep. So did my dolls. Galaxy didn't like the doctor—said all doctors lie. Nurses, too. But Gazelle said the nurses are nice. I never trusted Gazelle. She had a magic marker smile. The others left their faces blank. But it was White Lightning who screamed so loud, I swear I saw snowflakes in the ceiling. They fell so slowly through the air; some went up instead of down. I woke up gagging, the doctor sobbing by my side. "We thought we'd lost you," he said, adding, "anesthesia is not your friend." Anesthesia, I thought then, was a Russian princess or evil stepmother who poisoned me again and again.

After surgeries I look down and see myself as if I were another girl in the hospital bed below. *Other,* I call her, or *that little girl.* Like me, she sees with her left eye, then her right. Like feet, she trades them back and forth. If she selects both eyes, the world blurs. The angel who hovers at the base of the optic nerve is missing from mine/hers. Without an angel, there can be no third dimension. There is only Death in the shape of a giant black bird, waving his wings. I see him night after night. It's years before I realize only I can see him. And my nanny, Miss Mary, who dies the year I turn five.

My parents don't talk about it, so I don't either—the night I have to be rushed to the hospital, my fever climbing *103, 104, 105*, the fat-legged nurse with nylons that went *scratch-scritch* telling me I'm trying on a new dress as she snaps the hospital gown behind my neck. "Can I keep it?" I ask. "Yes, of course," she says, but she doesn't mean it. Grown-ups say a lot of things they don't mean. Like how there's nothing to worry about. I listen as the doctors and my parents speak in hushed voices, passing shadowy words back and forth: *seizures, delusions, brain damage.* My mother's face floats above me like a cloud while Death crouches in the corner, shifting his weight from one foot to the other. "Did you see him?" I asked my mother later. "He has a crow's head and wings, and he's taller than Daddy."

"Whatever you do," she hissed, "don't tell anyone else."

I never tell my mother about the night I died. She and my father were out for the night. My sister was babysitting, blasting rock 'n roll music in the living room. I still had a fever; my head throbbed. The stereo was right beneath my bed. I'd only heard classical music in our home, and I didn't like the beat of rock 'n' roll—it kept going faster and faster. When I looked up, I saw Death on the windowsill. "Go away," I whispered. He cocked his head and looked at me with one eye, then the other. *There's no need to worry,* I told myself. *He can't come into the room.* As if by invitation, he glided noiselessly through the glass and began circling. *It's okay. I'm dreaming,* I thought. *Mother says I can't die in my sleep.* He swooped down and pressed his great weight into my chest. I tried to scream, but no words came out. I tried to move, but my body turned to stone. I tried to breathe, but my mind went black. *I'm dead,* I thought after a while. *It's not so bad being dead.* When I opened my eyes, my pajamas were soaked with sweat. There was no music playing. The only sound was my heart racing. A pale light filled the room. I walked to the window and saw the full moon flooding the fields and hills as if everything were dressed in a bridal veil. I shivered. The fever, I realized, had broken.

"It's a gene," my mother says. "Call it the crazy gene. Some of us believe in unreal things. Some of us have visions. Some hear voices from the other side." She worries about the voices. She thinks I might be talking to them. "Sometimes you outgrow craziness," she says. "Sometimes not. Years ago, your cousin Bobby jumped in front of a train. The voices made him do it. The voices told him it's best to leave this world behind. He was just too sensitive for the world." I picture him. I hold his hand when he jumps.

But I never hear voices. I hope the silence will hold. Sometimes, after surgery, the other girl might hear a word or two. She answers or says things I'd never say. I don't care for her. When she opens her mouth, I press my fingers to her lips. "Hush now," I say. "No one wants to hear that."

The EKG machine beep-beeps before the nurse unhooks me and dresses me in a clean hospital gown, the snap cold at the base of my neck, and hands me a pill and a crinkly paper cup. "This'll make you sleepy," she says. "Sedatives don't work on me," I tell her. "My father used to give me Sominex. It makes me wild." But she doesn't listen. Soon the pill begins to sing a thready blue tune, first softly then louder. I rock from side to side on the bed and wave at attendants who push children on stretchers, at nurses in squeaky white shoes who guide trolleys of medicines between beds, at janitors who sweep the halls with wide brooms, at doctors with stethoscopes around their necks and clipboards, who speak to parents in low, somber voices. The clock arms glide past 10:00, 11:00, 12:00. *I want to run away,* I think and swing my legs over the edge of the bed. But I am wearing a hospital gown. *Where will I go without my clothes? And where is my mother?*

I flip back to the earliest pages I can read and find my mother in a twilight sleep, a doctor stationed between her legs. It's the day her last daughter is born, the umbilical cord wrapped so tightly around her infant's neck, the skin turns blue, then purple, then the color of dusk. Blood leaks into the baby's eyes as life slips from her every pore and rises as mist. *I am going home,* her soul thinks as it detaches from the flesh and looks back (this is why, in myths and dreams, one should never look back) just as the doctor tugs the child free from the womb with metal tongs. He holds her upside down and whacks her, once, twice, three times before she screams as air tears into her lungs. A nurse swaddles her in a pink blanket and places her in a bassinet. "Pink again?" my mother says when she opens her eyes. Then she closes them again. That's when Death stops in, looks down at me from above. *You?* he asks, cocking his head. *Here?*

Once upon a time, there was a girl who didn't want to be born. She was the last daughter of a gay man and an autistic woman. The woman insisted each of their children's births takes place in spring on a schedule that she wrote down. (My mother did everything on a schedule—even death.) The girl watched her siblings go first. "Don't leave me," she begged as they fell, helpless to the earth. There was a chill after each soul vanished. Still, she held back, not sitting too close to the edge. *Maybe they'll forget about me. Maybe they'll say they've had enough.* She figured she had at least a 50/50 chance. It's a wonder, really, any of them were born. But her parents wanted another son. They were barely speaking by the time her number was called. She remembers her father's lopsided grin, "I think we've done it again," the seed leaking onto her mother's pale thighs. The feeling her parents had then, something close to pride. Something closer to regret.

My Mother Was a Little Brown Bird

Fluttering around people in a state of constant agitation, terrified of being trapped, my mother was always opening windows and rushing out of doors "to catch a breath of fresh air." Even on a chilly October day with hurricane warnings, wind gusts combing the alfalfa fields. "What a lovely day!" she rhapsodized. "Who wants to go for a walk?" Not even the dogs followed her out the door. When my father came home from work, and she wasn't back yet, he sent Charles, the farmhand, to search for her. An hour later, as dusk was falling, Charles found her wandering aimlessly across the distant hills, gazing in wonder at what she called *Mother Nature's glorious show.* She didn't even notice the drenching rain, the tree limb sailing by her head, or the barn roof flying into the sky like a silver kite. Once inside, she ignored my father's glare, shook leaves and twigs from her hair, hopped over broken toys, crying children, beagles growling over an old bone on the living room carpet, and announced, "I'm starving!" She reached for a handful of peanuts, scattering shells as she walked, not seeing the family reflected in the black beads of her eyes.

No one ever hugged my mother, not my grandmother, not my sisters, not even my father, at least not after I was born. She cringed at hand holding, kissing, romance, and seduction in all its forms. One evening, at a cocktail party, I watched her shudder and run from a room when a man ran his speckled fingers across her bare arm, then leaned in close to tell her how lovely she looked in blue. She did look pretty—dressed in the silk gown and sapphire earrings my father had selected, a double string of pearls around her throat. "What a ghastly man," she said, her face flushed. "Putting his hands on me like that." I followed her to the cloakroom where she sat, gasping for air before grabbing her coat and running out into the night, a trail of feathers floating behind her.

"Don't," she'd say, pushing me back when I ran towards her, begging to be picked up. "You mustn't cling." If my mother relented and lifted me up in her arms, she insisted, "No kisses!" She shivered whenever she said the word *kiss*—she had a special aversion to the touch of lips. I learned to approach her gingerly like a stray cat. Not to look in her eyes. To slide quietly onto the green flowered couch beside her, scoot closer inch by inch. If I was sad, I didn't say so. Instead, I let the tears slip silently down my cheeks and sucked my thumb. On a good day, she might coo, "There, there," and pat my head. "Let's take that thumb out of your mouth. We don't want buck teeth now, do we?"

Twice a year my mother and I flew to Boston to visit my grandmother and to see the eye surgeon at Boston Children's Hospital. (I had five surgeries, spaced two or three years apart between the ages of one and fourteen.) It was always Winter Grandma who greeted us on crutches at the heavy door of her three-story mansion, then vanished without another word. After dropping off our suitcases and me, my mother took the cab back into Boston "to visit friends and see the sights of my childhood city." I'd peek in on Winter Grandma, but she was usually asleep in her antique mahogany bed, snoring like a beached walrus on a sea of twisted sheets. Sometimes she lifted her head and said weakly, "Go away. Can't you see I'm resting?" She wasn't the same as Summer Grandmother who counted the freckles on my nose, swam in her saltwater pool, rain or shine, and hid chocolates in every room of her summer house: Swiss chocolates wrapped in pictures of the Alps, Toblerone bars, and Droste apples she shared with me one slice at time "but only after you plié like a ballerina" or "do twenty jumping jacks" or "touch your toes with your nose."

"Is Grandma sad?" I asked my mother once. "Of course not," my mother snapped. "She's just old."

If I were sick or recovering from eye surgery with one eye patched, my mother would enter my room without a *hello* or *how are you*, sit in the corner rocking chair, and begin to read aloud. She didn't read children's stories or fairy tales (unless they were the original Brothers Grimm)—she couldn't tolerate "those ghastly saccharine endings." Instead, a Classics scholar, she chose a passage from the *Iliad* or the *Odyssey*, a Greek myth, or a tale of Ancient Athens and Sparta. "The Greek gods were just as unreasonable and cruel as our own," she would announce happily as Odysseus sailed further and further from his beloved Penelope who spent her life weaving and unravelling her husband's burial shroud. "Now that's a woman's life for you," she would sigh, adding "devotion is clearly over-rated." Sometimes, when she thought I wasn't listening, she would recite passages in Ancient Greek, the strange words like insects crawling into my thoughts and nesting in the dark hollows of my bones.

Like most birds, my mother was good at stuffing food down her children's gullets. She bragged that none of *her* children were picky eaters. "Open wide," she'd say, forking a giant piece of liver into my mouth. I learned to swallow without chewing, bypassing the tongue, consuming large amounts of food at great speed. I was not allowed to have opinions about taste or texture or appetite, or to leave the table without cleaning my plate. "One more bite," she'd say. And then, "Now, let's have another."

I remember my first day of kindergarten, sitting at my desk, holding my belly, round and hard as a basketball. I pressed into it with my thumbs, trying to release the pressure as I'd seen the vet do with our heifers that broke into the alfalfa field. "What happened to your stomach?" my teacher asked, peering down at me through silver-rimmed bifocals. "Oh, Mrs. Wallace," I said. "That's just breakfast. Wait till you see lunch."

My mother despised most other mothers, especially those who coddled and gushed over their children. She also disliked Dr. Spock— all that talk of treating your children with affection, pampering and applauding their every moment rather than training them properly. "Children are like dogs and heifers—what they need is discipline and a good routine," she said. "Besides, you don't want them to be attached to your apron strings forever. If you spoil them rotten, why would they ever leave home?"

The year she raised a seagull from a chick in our back yard, she complained about the fishy stench and poop all over the lawn. One day, when the bird was a few weeks old, she began hurling it from our porch. "This is how a fledgling learns to fly," she explained. We watched it drop like a stone again and again, day after day, until one morning the gull spread its wings, just before it hit the ground, swooped into the air, and flew away.

According to my mother, her children were *much* stronger than their suburban classmates—just as her Ayrshire cows were healthier than the Holsteins on neighboring farms. Never mind that I suffered from frequent fevers, flus, sore throats, night sweats, hallucinations, Rocky Mountain Spotted Fever, mumps, measles, pin worms, chicken pox, and some unidentified illness that kept me home from school for weeks at a time. Or that I was "a bit accident prone," as she put it. I was stung by swarms of bees, bitten by stray dogs, clawed by feral cats, bucked from horses, butted by a bull, and one morning, found unconscious on the side of the road by a truck driver who delivered me and my bicycle to the hospital. That afternoon, a doctor called my father and reported that an unidentified girl, who looked suspiciously like one of his, had been out cold in the ER since 9 a.m. Was he by chance missing a daughter?

"To think, you were in the hospital for seven hours, and we didn't notice your absence. But of course, it was you," my mother said, adding that even in sleep, I wasn't safe. I fell out of bed one night and knocked my front teeth out. My father brought me a bag of frozen peas wrapped in an old washcloth and said, "Bite on this until the bleeding stops." The peas got loose and rolled around my head and neck. I remember the taste of the blood and dishwater. And the peas, like the tips of icy fingers, pressing into my cheeks.

Home alone, when I was nine years old, I found in the back of my father's closet a box of love notes from a Naval officer, the pages as soft as tissue paper, the words faded and barely legible, each letter closing: *I will never forget you, Benjamin. My heart is forever yours.* Between the pages was a black and white photograph of a Naval officer; on the back—the date, 1944, inscribed *With love, Kenny.* The officer smiled at the camera, his face white, overexposed.

Later, when I asked my mother about the letters, she shrugged, "*That man* was the reason your father was dishonorably discharged from the Navy. Of course, *he* kept *his* job. A lot of men have affairs in the military. It's simply what happens. In the more enlightened warrior societies like Ancient Sparta, men were *expected* to take male lovers. The love between soldiers made them stronger on the battlefield. Sort of like Achilles and Patroclus in the *Iliad*, which I read aloud to you in the hospital."

"Once upon a time your father announced that he was cured," my mother explained. "This was long ago, on one of our last dates. I was a schoolteacher in Boston then, and he was living in New York City, doing some kind of conversion therapy, seeing a real quack. We were dining at the automat, Horn & Hardart; I'd selected the meatloaf and baby braised carrots. He was eating Salisbury steak with a side of creamed spinach. I handed him a napkin—his lips were green. 'Cured?' I asked. 'Isn't that what you do to a ham?' He didn't laugh. After supper he asked me to marry him—got down on one knee beside the table. It was so embarrassing. I suppose he was trying to be romantic. I said yes, as long as he was certain he could produce offspring. This was the late 40's. A lot of women married homosexuals back then."

My mother stabbed a forkful of roast beef, then wiped her mouth with a napkin and ran upstairs to find a pen to write a note to herself. "I keep forgetting to call the vet," she explained as she sat back down. "One of the cows has mastitis." She nibbled her cornpone before the phone rang, and she leapt up. "I have to take this call. It might be about that Canadian bull semen I've been trying to import." "Sit!" my father screamed, pounding the table with his fist, his iced tea spilling, the glass smashing on the tile floor. "Eat!" My mother froze in mid-air, her eyes glazing into the distance that was always there between my parents like a sacred room no one else entered. I pictured it as a paperweight full of snow—a tiny foreign land where princes and princesses fell asleep but never woke. Where no one ever kissed or rescued them.

"I have a baby cow," I bragged in first grade. For *Show and Tell*, I brought a curry comb and brush to class, demonstrated how to bathe and groom an invisible calf. "You wet and brush her coat forward and upward at a thirty-degree angle to make the hair grow faster," I explained. "You know she likes it when her ears glide forward. You know she loves you when she licks you with her long, pink sandpaper-tongue." Dried milk and cow spit smeared my jacket. Manure and straw stuck in my shoe treads. "You stink," my classmates said.

"Consider this photo of Miss America," my mother told my 4-H class. "She's a model girl from northern European stock with blue eyes, clear skin, rosy cheeks, and blond hair, tied back in a ribbon or a headband to show off her pretty face. Notice how Miss America is slender, but not too slender, tall but not too tall. She might take ballet lessons to improve her posture so that she walks gracefully with her shoulders pressed back, her neck long, her young but promising chest pressed forward and displayed in modest yet tastefully revealing clothing. In public she is trained to smile and laugh easily, showing off her even white teeth when she says, *yes, please*, and *thank you so very much*. Her fine manners and good health are esteemed social values.

A show cow, much like this young woman, is an ideal specimen of her breed with nice coloring, ideally white with reddish brown spots arranged in a pleasing pattern, a robust but not too robust frame and good symmetry, her tail placed equidistant between her hip bones and curry-combed to show that it is shiny and not coarse. Trained to walk calmly around the show ring, to stop and pose with her legs spread evenly apart and firmly planted, she lifts her head for the judge to admire the smooth line from her long, shaved neck to her shoulders and ribs, and onto the withers and the hook and pin bones. One hind leg is placed approximately six inches in front of the other to show off the width, depth, and teat placement of her well-shaped udder. She eats grass and grains and, when mature, weighs approximately 1200 pounds. One day, this ideal specimen will produce an ample milk and calf crop.

"The model bull," my mother added "is of little use. All a dairy farmer really needs from a bull is best kept in cold storage."

"Little girls shouldn't own bulls," my father said the day Melvin, a sickly red calf was born. "Besides, we don't keep bulls on the dairy farm." But my mother disagreed. "Why not? Melvin can be her own personal bull."

That was the year of the drought. Not a drop of rain fell in July and August, and heat lightning lit up the sky night after night. The alfalfa flowered early and then turned brown, dropping its leaves, and the red dirt cracked and hardened like cement. My parents fought about the price of feed, the Vietnam War, what they would do if my brother was drafted, and my love affair with a baby bull. "Are you going to be the one to explain it to her when the time comes?" my father asked. "She's a farm girl," my mother shrugged, tossing her head.

My siblings were away at camp or at the beach with friends. Bored and lonesome, I stayed awake night after night, planning to run away. I'd take Melvin, as soon as he was healthy, and Mom's Mastercard. I imagined staying at a Howard Johnson's where I could sneak Melvin into my room without going through the lobby.

Melvin grew strong, and by fall he weighed five hundred pounds. I played tag with him after school, waving burlap bags like flags. Melvin charged and charged, stopping short in a cloud of dirt. Once he accidentally butted me into the air, then nuzzled me apologetically when I lay on the ground.

I wrote stories for Miss Tabb, my third-grade teacher, in which Melvin was the star, and illustrated them during class. I can still see Melvin galloping through the pages of my mind. He spears murderers and thieves with his horns and outruns wolves and cop cars. When I'm tired, he lets me ride on his back. Miss Tabb said girls don't ride bulls. Bulls won't allow it. But she never met Melvin, my own personal bull.

I came home from a school camping trip, and Melvin was gone. My father said Melvin had been sent to another farm where there were other bulls and cows his own size for him to play with. My mother said, "Your father tells lies."

We ate steak night after night. My mother chewed happily, wiping the grease on her napkin. "They say that love makes the meat rich and sweet," she said. "It's true! Isn't that so?"

"Hello, Melvin," I whispered before kissing my steak. My father pushed his plate away and turned white. "Don't talk to your food!" he shouted. I stabbed another forkful of pink meat, held it up to the light. "Don't you look lovely tonight?" I asked. Then I took another bite.

I still dream I'm at one of my childhood birthday parties, and my mother, a whistle around her neck, sings out my classmates' names and checks them off a list: "Amy Sloane, Stephanie Combs, Nina Dubrovnik, Ginny Semmes, Teddy Crawford." In grade school my mother insisted on inviting the whole class over to our stone farmhouse. She took down the fly strips in the kitchen and hung party balloons from the gate at the bottom of our dirt driveway and planned an afternoon of party games. I see the children's faces glowing like pale moons. Even the dead ones light up when my mother calls their names. *Make them go home,* I whisper, just as I did when I was a girl. But my mother never listens. Amy Sloane, the girl who pinches me and calls me Freak, wins the sack race. Nina Dubrovnik bursts into tears when she trips on a rock in the egg and spoon race. Teddy's tooth falls out when he's eating cake. I sit under the tulip poplar watching my mother hand out ribbons and goody bags. After the guests leave, my mother teaches me how to write thank-you notes at the kitchen table. *Thank you for the Christmas Barbie*, I write. *I like her red velvet dress. Thank you for the movie-star Barbie. I like her sunglasses and gold purse. Thank you for Ken. I like his bathing trunks and comb-lined head.* When the notes are finished and addressed, I bury my presents in the sandbox and make tombstones out of cardboard, inscribing each one with magic marker. *Here lies Summer Barbie in her blue striped swimsuit. Here lies Go-Go Barbie in her black boots. Here lies Teddy Crawford's tooth.*

I was in sixth grade when I curled Stephanie Comb's hair around my colored pencils in English class. My teacher, Mrs. Ward, tapped me on the shoulder with her orange fingernails. "Come with me," she hissed and pulled me into the hallway. "You have to stop touching that girl's hair. I'm beginning to worry you're a lesbian." She sent a note home that day—carefully tucked in an envelope with the inscription: *A private matter for Mrs. (not Mr.) Heyward to discuss with Nin.*

"All little girls are lesbians," my mother said, tossing the note in the trash basket. "Were you a lesbian?" I asked. "I was—a *little* lesbian," she said. "I had crushes on girls. But I wasn't *really* lesbian." "How do you know?" I asked. She shrugged. "It's just like the heifers. They start humping each other in the springtime." "Cows are lesbians?" I asked. "It's genetic," she said. "Some of us get more of the lesbian, some, less. Time will tell how much of the lesbian you possess." "How will it tell?"

My mother sighed, her silver-blue glasses sliding down her nose. "If you are in your twenties, and you still want to play with Stephanie's hair . . . Well, then, you're a lesbian."

"Not a hairdresser?" I asked. My mother stared at me blankly.

"I do hope you're not a hairdresser."

"**Sex Education** is a total waste of time," my mother said. If the heifers can figure it out, certainly you girls can, too."

"I think your wife has that syndrome—defined by a certain Dr. Asperger," my father's friend, the minister said, rattling the ice in his cocktail glass. My father had been complaining about my mother's "proclivities and peculiarities," her aversion to cooking, cleaning house, intimate conversation, cocktail parties, dresses, high heels, everyday pleasantries, and her habit of wearing L.L. Bean boots and stained trousers to town. No matter how hard he tried to teach her, she could never select a flattering lipstick. Once, he sent his secretary to *Rose's Drug and Gifts* to buy my mother lipstick, and she selected a tube of Revlon's *Cherries in the Snow.* Ever since, my mother wore that same bright shade, day and night—a defiant slash of red mimicking her mouth.

"You're right. She rarely looks well-groomed," the minister nodded, adding, "autism runs in families. Her brother, you said, was institutionalized at one point?" My father stood up quickly, a red wave rising up his neck. "My wife is not a syndrome. She's from New England is all. She's like a saltwater lobster in a hot Virginia pond." He ushered the minister out of the house.

The minister didn't know the family rule. Only my father was allowed to criticize my mother.

Asperger's Symptom 1: Repetitive motor patterns such as hand flapping or arm waving

"*As a girl,*" my mother said, "*I used to flap my arms and spin like a top. I loved twirling faster and faster. 'Stop that!' your grandmother said. 'Stop that right now.' I kept on until I lay on the ground, the sky whirling with me.*"

Asperger's Symptom 2: Inflexibility and over-adherence to, or dependence on, routines

"*I like to live my life with a schedule. And a meal plan. If tomorrow is Tuesday, I want to know I will have lunch at 12:30 PM—a porkchop with apples and a side of collard greens.*"

Asperger's Symptom 3: A difficulty socializing and obsessive interests in specific topics, which may be of little interest to others

"*I was happy until I turned eleven, and suddenly all the girls started giggling and acting idiotic around boys. And going on endless shopping sprees to buy clothes. I don't know why they needed so many clothes! That's when I became interested in cows and baseball. I can still recite the ERAs of my favorite Red Sox pitchers. And the milk production rates for each of our lactating cows.*"

Asperger's Symptom 4: A dislike of being touched

"I just hate it when people think they can hug or kiss you. Who gave them permission to do that? That's what I dislike about visiting friends in Europe. The French! The Italians!"

Asperger's Symptom 5: Unusual reactions to social settings

"I despise restaurants. So many wives think it's nice to go out to eat at The Angus Barn with their husbands. What's nice about sitting in a frigid room, waiting forever for a steak that might or might not be cooked to your liking, and staring at your spouse? I'd rather stay home and enjoy my meal."

Asperger's Symptom 6: A lack of maternal instinct

"If you're going to have children, hire babysitters. Hire them as soon as you know you're pregnant. Your child is going to bore you to tears, and vice versa—especially the newborns. Infancy is what I call the grub stage of life. The more help you hire, the happier you'll both be."

Asperger's Symptom 7: Lack of empathy

"Ginny, my suburban neighbor walked her dachshund up our farm road the other day, and my Rottweiler killed it. He didn't mean to, but his jaws are too strong. 'It was just a dog,' I tried to tell her. Not that a wiener dog is really a dog."

Asperger's Symptom 8: A difficulty with relationships

"The first years of marriage were difficult, but your father and I got used to each other. Like the fox and the Little Prince, we tamed each other—or made arrangements. He had his special friends. And I kept my cows. He never did like the heifers."

Asperger's Symptom 9: A difficulty expressing love

"People nowadays always say, 'I love you.' So schmaltzy. I would never say I love you. But I am fond of you."

Hired Hands

My father was a man of secrets, or, as he put it, "I don't like folks knowing our business." When he discovered I wanted to be a writer, he gave me a list of things not to write about, explaining "some stories you best keep to yourself." The list grew long over the years. "Whatever you do," he told me, "Don't embarrass us. Don't tell my stories. And don't write about race or class. Don't ever mention anyone who is black or Mexican or Native American or poor white. In other words, don't write about the hired hands—the babysitters, the gardeners, and the men who worked in the barn. No one needs to hear about them.

"Above all, don't mention your black nanny, or people will think you're a spoiled brat, a modern-day Scarlett O'Hara. Besides, Miss Mary insisted she wasn't black—or colored as the word was then. She was part-Native American, part-white, and part-African. She had her own name for herself. Don't write or say it aloud. Don't mention any of those racist slurs you grew up hearing. Miss Mary had a whole litany of swear words and slang. You're a young lady, and you should write like one if you want to garner respect. Write as if you were raised by your mother, not Miss Mary, not that pack of farmhands you ran around with like a feral hound."

"The day Miss Mary arrived, she rode up to the house in a Yellow Cab, knocked on the door, said she'd heard a white lady was having babies like popcorn. She reckoned the missus might be needing a hand with the chillens," my father said. "We'd had three babies in four years, and your sister Louisa was well on her way. I kept thinking we'd be finished after four with all the diapers and carrying on. But your mother and I kept hoping the next one would be a boy. By the time you were born, your mother was worn-out. So was I. We handed you over to Miss Mary full-time. As an infant, you slept in her arms, ate with her in the kitchen, and cried inconsolably when she went to the Baptist church on Sunday mornings. She called you Little Pea when you behaved, Son of a Bird when you were naughty. Whenever she lost track of you, we'd hear her hollering, 'Ain't nobody seen hide nor hair of my little Son of a Bird?' After a while, the farmhands called you Son of a Bird too."

For years I was afraid to write about my past. I'd think, *my father's right—some stories are best left untold.* But then there was a summer afternoon in Virginia when memory opened like the pages of a book. And I missed being someone else. Or the child who picked peas with her nanny in the July heat. Who was carried in her large black arms back to the house where they shucked peas in the kitchen, a fan blowing fly strips overhead, Miss Mary humming hymns, calling her "Little Pea," dragging her thumb down the pods, splitting them in half, the peas bouncing in a silver bowl. The girl asked, "Which little pea am I?" The nanny laughed and smacked her thigh. "You a funny little pea. The funniest, specialest little pea—that's the pea you is."

Still, I worry, who wants to read a racist memory—one that begins with a white child in a black nanny's arms? Should I refuse to write about it? How, in the mornings, we carried a pail of breakfast scraps ("the nasty stinkin slop," she called it) to the pigs, gathered eggs, dug potatoes in the garden, hung clothes on the line, me handing Miss Mary the pins. Before eleven, she carried me upstairs for a nap and sat beside my bed sipping Pepsi. "Shut your eyes," she said. And I did. When I peeked, she was open-mouthed, asleep, her breasts rising and falling inside her starched cotton dress. I played with my doll babies until Miss Mary woke and announced, "I just had me a little beauty rest."

I remember another day in Little Pea's life when my father caught me hiding in the loft after I snuck out of the house during naptime. Lying on my back on top of the haybales, I watched mud daubers build their clay nests, barn swallows flying in and out, straw in their beaks. "How many times do I have to tell you not to play up here!" my father shouted before dragging me down the ladder, pulling down my pants, and smacking me. *Whap-whap*. When I looked up, Miss Mary was running down the hill beneath the mimosa trees. "What you doing to that child?" she screamed and snatched me from my father's arms and pressed me against her chest, her body slick with perspiration and rage. The whole way back to the house, she muttered under her breath, "Damn white folks—don't even know how to raise they own chillens."

Is it racist to imitate Miss Mary's accent and vernacular? Is there a point where racism begins and ends, a line I can be careful never to cross? I want badly to say *no* and then *yes*. So I call Miss Mary back from the dead. She looks so tired when she arrives, her hair in a net, sweat beading on her forehead as she fishes ice cubes from her water glass and drops them inside her blouse. "Cooling my chest," she called it. We had no AC in 1963. How hot it was then! Hot enough to hatch an egg without a hen. Like Otis, our baby rooster, who pecked his way out of an egg in the basket on the kitchen counter. Afterwards, Otis and I followed Mary wherever she went. She said, "You both mistaken me for your mamas."

I know what you're thinking. Miss Mary wasn't just a nanny. She was a cook, a laundress, a housekeeper, a savior, a saint. I needed her then, even after she passed. Miss Mary was my protector, mother, first love, goddess. I felt her like a song, a longing, an ache. I kept her close as a breath. Even now, when I sit down to write in the morning, I ask Miss Mary how she is. Miss Mary says what she always said, "I'm blessed, Child. I bless you, too." It's a little ritual we do.

But I think it's time I asked her permission. "Is it okay for you to be here? In these poems and stories?" Miss Mary stares at me aghast. "Good Lawd, child," she says. "I'm 118 years old if I'm a day. An old southern ghost. Do you think I get to pick where I stay?" She shakes her head. "Ain't nobody choosing the time, the skin, the heart you gonna live on in. Not me, not you, Little Pea. Not your daddy neither. That old SOB."

At night I lay awake, listening to the grandfather clock tick, the radiators hiss, certain that somewhere inside or behind them, something was lurking. Scared, I raced downstairs on sock feet and climbed into Miss Mary's bed, curling against the soft curve of her back. I turned and wiggled and turned and wiggled until she woke.

"It's watching me again, Miss Mary," I said.

"What?"

"I don't know."

"You got to name it," Miss Mary said. "That way it don't scare you no more. Talk to it, too."

"And say what?"

"Say: Don't bother me no more. Little Pea be needing her sleep now. Say it quiet so Miss Mary gets her rest."

"Little Pea be needing her sleep now," I whispered as I stared at the ceiling. "That's me. Little Pea. She be needing her sleep, don't bother Little Pea, sleeping now . . ."

Some nights I woke up screaming so loud, I woke the whole house. Even the beagles began to howl. I saw Death pressing against my window and was certain he was coming inside. "He's right there," I sobbed when Miss Mary came running. When I pointed him out, she rushed at the window, waving her large black hands. "He's gone now," she said. And he was! Miss Mary had magic hands. "Son of a Bird," she sighed when she rocked me back to sleep. "My little Son of a Bird." But Death came back. Death always comes back.

If Miss Mary were sick or had a few nights off, Death knew I was his. He would land on my sill as soon as the house went dark and tilt his head from one side to the other, seeing me with his left eye then his right. Sometimes he opened his wings and flew. I did, too. But my wings were too small, and I had trouble staying aloft. Like the seagull my mother raised that summer in Maine and taught to fly by flinging it off the porch, laughing when it plummeted again and again, I swooped up and up, then plunged downward, flapping my skinny arms until I fell off the bed and knocked my front teeth out. "The toothless wonder," my father called me before my grown-up teeth grew in.

After Miss Mary left one day and never returned (it was years before I learned she was dead), my mother dropped me off at the barn with the one-armed farmhand and Korean war veteran, Mr. Shaver. "If a farmhand can look after heifers, he can look after you, too," she said before driving off in a cloud of dust. Mr. Shaver was leaning against the red farm truck, smoking, eyeing me up and down. "Now what're we gonna do with you?" he asked. When I started to sob, he patted my head, "Aww, hush now, it's all right little gal. Look, I got something for ya." He slid his artificial arm out of his sleeve and handed it to me—showed me how to screw in the fork and knife attachments, fishing dirty marshmallows out of his pocket with his oil-stained hand. I sat in the grass and stabbed the marshmallows with the fork and knife, and watched Mr. Shaver's son, Bud, muck stalls. Mr. Shaver smoked Marlboros or chewed on the sweet ends of meadow grass and talked. He asked me, did I want to toss horseshoes or learn to blow tunes on a pop bottle. And was Jesus my friend? I shook my head and held onto his arm, rocking it like a baby doll.

At mealtimes, Mr. Shaver walked me to the house, still cradling his plastic arm. "Can I have it?" I asked. "Naw," he said, "You can borrow it if you keep it nice." He didn't care for the arm himself, said it was gift from his Uncle Sam, but it never did attach right. My mother wouldn't allow the prosthesis inside. She made me leave it on the doorstep. When she wasn't looking, I snuck it upstairs, gave it a bath, some lunch, a good long nap. But when I woke, the arm had fallen out of the bed and lay on the floor, a wasp crawling over the sunlit pink fingers. I saw it for what it was then—an ugly thing, a container for silverware, an alien, the rest of it gone back to the moon.

Mr. Shaver never did a lick of work, according to my father, but he liked to hunt. And we had a groundhog problem, our pastures riddled with holes. My father didn't want anyone shooting around the horses and heifers, but after his broodmare stepped in a groundhog hole and broke her leg, he changed his mind and asked Mr. Shaver to get rid of the varmints anywhere, anyhow. Mr. Shaver and Bud and I spent the days when it didn't rain killing groundhogs.

Mr. Shaver would whistle up his pack of hounds, and we'd head for the fields and pour creek water down the woodchuck holes, the dogs sniffing and baying and wagging their tails. A groundhog would pop his head up nearby, and a beagle would seize and shake it, the groundhog whipping back and forth, nipping the dogs and squealing, blood and fur-bits flying through the air. If one got loose and ran, Mr. Shaver shot it. Called himself one-shot Freddie. He never missed. He invited me to a barbecue at night—said woodchuck tastes like squirrel tastes like raccoon tastes like rabbit tastes like possum tastes like chicken. *Don't matter what it is if you sauce it up nice.*

I followed Dr. Flynn, the vet, whenever he visited the barn, asking a stream of questions, catching cats that needed to be neutered, soothing dogs when he gave them shots, corralling calves into the chute with the head-lock gate for dehorning—blood squirting from the heifers' heads like a fountain. He taught me to dust their wounds with styptic powder, spray them with fly and maggot repellant, and observe them for days afterward for signs of infection. One spring my yellow tabby kitten, Lorna Doone, caught distemper, one eye oozing puss, the other sealed shut. He said to ice the closed eye twice a day. I held the kitten in my lap with a bag of frozen peas pressed to her head at dawn and dusk until one afternoon her cornea fell out and rolled in the sawdust—a tiny ball of transparent Jell-O.

There were two farmhouses my parents rented, one to a fastidious bachelor named Mr. Love and another to the Shavers. The bachelor's house was white stone and so covered with roses, I thought the stones bloomed. And his grass was always freshly mowed and looked hand-combed. The farmhands' yard was red clay with dead cars and rusty tractor parts, a horse-shoe pit, a grill, and a table with white plastic chairs where they ate and played the banjo on summer nights. Sometimes I'd fall asleep to the music. One night my father and I went down to watch. "Come on and dance," they said. I hopped and jumped until my feet ached. They called me grasshopper. "Dance, little grasshopper. You dance!"

Bud had a cousin my age, Penny Sue, with yellow hair permed into tiny ringlets like Shirley Temple. She came to the farm, dragging a bag of Wonder Bread, wadding the bread into balls and stuffing them in her cheeks. When no one was looking, she rubbed a slice in the dirt and popped it in her mouth, then handed me a piece. I folded it over, scooped up some wet sand, and made myself a dirt sandwich. She showed me the different flavors of dirt: red clay and black compost and leafy brown garden soil. We tasted them all, and a few days later, I had pin worms. I felt them in my butt and could see them in the toilet, white parentheses gliding out into the water. My mother found them in my sheets, too, and took a few to the doctor on a piece of Scotch tape. The doctor prescribed Pin-X, wrote a script for the whole family. Even the dogs took Pin-X.

Drive-by kitties, Mr. Shaver called them—the cats tossed from car windows when people drove by our farm. On any given year we had between thirty and fifty barn cats. "How many cats ya'll got now?" Penny Sue liked to ask. We were learning to count, but we never could count them all. The number changed all the time—many new arrivals didn't survive. Some were run over by the mower in the alfalfa field, crouching low instead of fleeing when the long blade swept the tall grass. Others were killed by dogs, and still others died from respiratory illnesses. I dug cat graves in the soft dirt behind the chicken coop and marked them with twigs and stones. If I didn't bury them deep enough, the dogs dug them up and carried them around like chew toys.

Everyone liked my sister, Sal, especially Bud. He followed her everywhere like a scent hound. If she didn't come to the barn after school, he'd be asking me, "Where's your pretty sister?" Or "Run on up to the house and see if Sal wants a tractor ride." Or "Tell Sal I found a new litter of kittens in the loft." I did sometimes, just to watch Bud blush and stutter, words sticking to his tongue. He was always giving her gifts: four-leaf clovers, daisies in a Mason jar, a baby rabbit, a gold necklace with a heart. Mostly, he stared at the dirt, afraid she might laugh or tease him like the rest of us. But Sal just let him blush. And dream. Like she didn't know yet what kind of cruelty her beauty was.

The summer I turned five, my father decided to teach the farmhands to read. I lay on my belly in the loft and peeked through the broken slats, spying on them. Writing with yellow chalk on the green blackboard that hung outside the tack room, my father, an architect, drew perfect geometric letters, each a little building I wanted to crawl inside.

Every day he lined the letters up: A, AT, BAT. "Understand?" he asked. "Anyone want to write CAT?" He handed the chalk to one of the men who ran his fingers through his oiled hair, leaving tracks like a plowed field. "Can't teach this old dog," he said and nodded at Bud standing beside him. "That young'un neither. Right Buddy Boy?"

Sixteen years old, Bud blushed, shame scalding his skin. He'd been working on the farm since he was twelve. I remember the day he hid in the hayloft when the truant officer stopped by. "You seen that Shaver boy?" he asked me. I shook my head, "No Sir." "You know it's a sin to lie?" he asked, eyeing me suspiciously. "Yes, Sir. But I haven't seen hide nor hair of Bud Shaver," I shrugged, lifting my palms to the sky.

Bud's back curled forward like a question mark. I wondered if he was crying. "Don't worry, Son," my father said. Then he wrote on the board, I SIT IN SHIT. He read the words out loud. The men burst out laughing. "That word's sheee-it?" Bud asked, pointing at the chalkboard. My father nodded and explained that SH makes a *shhh* sound.

That's when, before my eyes, the letters became words became meaning. Like haybales, I could move them around to build a fort, or a house with windows and doors. I couldn't wait for the men to leave, when I'd climb down the ladder and slide the saddle-washing stool beneath the chalkboard, balance on the soap-sticky wood, and write an I, an IN, a NIN. Then erase them and start all over again.

One of the last times I saw Bud was an afternoon in April, a spring day so hot, all the petals fell off the tulips and blew across the alfalfa field in gusts. The beagles lay under the sweetgum tree, panting—didn't even lift their heads when I whistled. I'd just come home from school, was still wearing a plaid kilt and navy socks; my white button-down blouse stuck to my back. Bud was mucking out horse stalls. I didn't know it was only days before he'd leave for bootcamp, then Vietnam. That in a week I'd run around the farm, searching for him, calling his name. He handed me the pitchfork. "Gimme a hand," he said. "I'm done in." He leaned against the doorjamb. "You know it's my birthday? I'm eighteen today."

"Happy birthday," I said, spearing a manure ball. "Whatcha gonna do about it?" "Gonna fuck my gal," he said with a smirk. "See here?" He reached into his pocket, pulled out a picture, and handed it to me. I'd never heard him say fuck before. I tossed my ponytail like it was no big deal and stared at the picture: a blond lady bent over, her eyes shut tight, the wind filling her skirt, exposing her underwear. "Yep, I'm gonna fuck my gal. Then I'll fuck Sal."

"Nuh-uh," I said. "You're nothing but a big fat shitball!" I crumpled the picture in my hand, threw the pitchfork at him, and took off running, past the sawdust heap, around the barn, behind the chicken coop, him closing in on me, wheezing hard. "Big fat shitball!" I called out as I dodged him and doubled back. He caught ahold of my shirt and yanked me to the ground. "What'd you call me?" "Shitball, shitball!" I screamed. He punched me in the mouth.

“Don’t you ever call me that again,” he said, striding away. “Shitball,” I shouted and ran for the house, licking blood from my lips.

My father put his fingers in my mouth. “Your teeth are hanging on tight. You just need to gargle is all.” I showed him the creased picture of Bud’s gal. “That’s Marilyn Monroe,” he said. That lady killed herself in ‘62.” I stared at Marilyn—the look on her face like a warning, like she was leaning forward behind bars. “Bite me,” she hissed. I wanted to, but my mouth hurt too bad. I licked my swollen lips and tasted blood and salt. I spat. And spat again.

“Marilyn,” I said back. “This is all your fault.”

A Lady, a Gentleman and Two Strange Birds

"The past is gone and you can't get it back," my father always said. But I want to tell him, *you can still visit*. The farmland is there, and my mother's shadow lingers in the doorway of the stone house. I can see her now, tilting her head, as if listening for the songs of the heifers in the fields, the horses in their stalls, the Rottweilers and beagles in the front yard under the tulip poplars, the thirty stray cats in the hayloft or sleeping in the sun, the six sows in the sty before we ate them, one by one, the bantam rooster and his nine hens before the red fox picked them off, running across the alfalfa field each morning with a fresh kill in his mouth. Gone, too, is the parakeet my father kept in the tack room, the parakeet that died from heatstroke or lack of water and once, a peanut, and was always replaced by an identical yellow-green budgie who dehydrated or was cooked on a July day so hot, the barn was a frying pan with the lid on tight. (After a while, I never knew which parakeet was in the cage—Tony or Tanya or Tina or Tulip or Tallulah.) And the bees my father kept in wooden hives that flew through the holes in our screens and drowned in our cocktail glasses. The black racers and rat snakes that slithered across the floorboards in our attic. Snakes, according to my mother, were better than the Orkin man at keeping the rodent population down. I lay awake at night, listening to the *swish-swish* overhead, the sound like ladies' skirts sweeping the floor as they danced.

Our house began as a stone square. My father, an architect, added two wings onto it to accommodate the ever-expanding family. By the time I, the last child of six, arrived, it was shaped like a U. Children's bedrooms were on the two sides of the U so we could look out our windows and see each other getting dressed. "I see you naked," one sister would call out through an open window. Another yelled back, "I see you in your polka-dotted underpants!" From 7:00 to 8:50, I watched my sisters doing their homework, framed in the yellow light. At 9:00 sharp, the house went dark, the day ending with a flick of the switch—like a movie without credits. I lay back in bed and listened as the night sounds began: horses kicked their stall doors; tree frogs clung to the window screens and sang to one another; owls screeched and swooped over the fields, and the rooster crowed and crowed—my father said that was because he was an Andalusian rooster and came from the wrong time zone.

The only time the lights came back on in the night was when one of us took sick. I'd sit up in bed and listen after a sister cried out, "I don't feel good!" My mother never woke—she slept through screams, thunderstorms, howling dogs, ringing phones, strangers, and policemen knocking on the door. My father, half-asleep, drifted into our bedrooms on sock feet. In one hand he held a glass of water, and in the other, a Bayer aspirin. He believed in Bayer, owned stock in the company, said it cured everything—nausea, diarrhea, flu, canker sores, nightmares, pink eye, insomnia. "Take this," he'd say. "You'll feel much better." If one pill didn't work, he'd give you another. I can still feel the little pill entering my bloodstream like a tiny white tooth.

Come spring our farm turned green overnight. Peepers started to sing, and the flowering began, the hills turning red and white and pink, pollen coating the air in a yellow sheen, everyone starting to sneeze. Our male dogs ran off, following the scent of bitches in heat. With no bulls in our fields, the heifers humped one another. Geldings whinnied and bucked and trotted along the fence lines as mares sidled up to them on the other side, lifting and swishing their tails. The neighborhood carpool driver, Mrs. Humphries, wouldn't give us rides anymore—not after she stopped her station wagon one afternoon and waited for Tigger and Teensy Weensy, our two tabby cats, to finish mating in the middle of the road. "Cover your eyes girls," Mrs. Humphries said. She didn't want to expose her daughters "to all the indecent goings-on." University students drove up our dirt road day and night, pulled over by the fields, and tore off their clothes as they ran through the tall grass. Abandoned shirts hung on barbed wire fences; panties dangled from cattails. My horse stopped just short of trampling a couple on an afternoon ride. The pier on the trout pond was a favorite spot. If I wanted to swim, I let the Rottweiler scare lovers off. Usually, they dove into the lake's cool green water, swam around naked till I asked if they were getting bit yet. The trout were always hungry. They nibbled pendulous body parts.

Summer days, I lazed in the tall grass and watched buzzards float overhead, wondering whose carcass they'd pick clean next. I listened to cicadas sing, pulled their hollow shells from the bark of hickory trees. I built hay forts, and once, stole the burger out of Bud's lunch sack, replaced it with a cowpie (this was the day after he gave me a fat mouth). And I got more whuppings than I could count. After a while I didn't feel a sting. I learned not to look my father in the eye. Not to beg. Not to cry. Before he even asked, I said, "Nope, I didn't do it. I wasn't playing in the hayloft. I didn't touch Bud's burger. I would never ever steal a lollipop from the candy jar," even if a chewed stick was hanging from my mouth. I said, "Penny Sue, gave it to me." Or "my swim teacher, Miss Patsy, said it was mine—for swimming the butterfly." "Is that why I saw you climbing on the stool, fishing in my sweets jar?" he asked. "Must have been someone else," I shrugged. "Must have been," he smirked, a way-off look in his eyes. Like he was trying to decide how much he wanted to smack me. Or how much he admired a liar like himself.

My father often joked that he was the father of one lady, a gentleman, two girls, and two strange birds—in that order.

Lisa, the first, was the only lady in the house—she came from another planet where people washed their hair and hands and listened when he talked. She was the only sister with a room of her own. She stayed in that room with the door closed, dolls lined up on her bed, china animals arranged on a shelf above her desk, not one of them broken, not a dust mote settling on anything she owned. Even her closet was organized with her shoes, clean and polished, no manure in the treads, her dresses and blouses, pressed and hanging from smallest to largest. I wasn't allowed to enter—not until I was old enough not to mess up her things. She said she wondered why Mom never taught us proper hygiene. Once, after I knocked on her door, she pulled a tick that was hanging behind my ear like a fat brown pearl.

The gentleman and second born, Jimmy, was sent away to prep school after eight years at one of the all-white private schools in town where he clowned around so much, he never learned to read properly—or that was how my mother explained it. (This was long before *learning disability* became a common diagnosis.) When he was given the SSATs, the standardized tests for prep school admission, he scored so low, she wondered if the circles were misaligned. She blamed his teachers. "All that money down the drain," she sighed, adding, "he was never Harvard-bound." My father insisted that he just didn't apply himself. "If it were one of the girls who struggled in school, I wouldn't have worried," he said. "Girls, after all, don't need to make it in the world." My mother nodded, adding that I had been their last hope for a replacement son, someone who could follow in my father's footsteps. Before I was born, my name was George.

The favorite child, number three, was Sal with her squinty grin, her head cocked to one side, her auburn hair pinned back in tortoise-shell barrettes—she was the first sister allowed to grow her bangs. The rest of us had the same haircuts—bobs with bangs, cut every month at Watson's Beauty School where novice beauticians practiced on us. "How come Sal is allowed to grow her hair?" "How come Sal gets to go horseback riding with Dad before school?" "Why is Sal always sitting in the front seat?" "Because she's nice," my father said, "unlike the rest of you girls." In school, she won all those prizes for teachers' pet. Spirit awards, they called them. Or best all-around athlete or pupil or smile. Behind her back, I called her Tinkerbelle.

"Let's go to the barn!" my mother said every day after school, pushing us out the door before we unzipped our jackets. Everyone except Louisa, who stayed behind on the green flowered couch in the living room, kicking one leg, twirling her hair, reading *Little Women* for the hundredth time. She didn't own a calf, didn't like horseback riding, didn't feed the pigs or chickens, didn't build hay forts, and never mucked stalls. "How come Louisa is allowed to stay inside? Why doesn't she do barn chores?" I asked. "Louisa is not a farm child. She's a genetic anomaly—sort of like Stuart Little," my mother explained. "That's the thing about motherhood—you never know what or who is going to come out of you."

L'enfant sauvage was my mother's nickname for Julie, the fifth-born child. "She could have been raised by wolves," she said. Julie lived in the woods, adopted baby birds and snakes, bringing them home to raise. As soon as she was old enough, my mother sent her to nature camp in the Blue Ridge Mountains. When she returned, Julie announced that her favorite classes were taxidermy and snake handling. She spent our summer vacation in Maine picking up snakes and searching for dead animals. We'd be driving along the highway, and she'd spot a carcass and shout STOP at the top of her lungs. My mother called these *roadkill sightings*. The Ford Falcon would screech to a halt. Julie would climb out of the car to inspect a dead deer, raccoon, or squirrel. Usually, the dead weren't fresh enough. "It's kind of like selecting vegetables or fruit," she explained. "You want the dead to be just right." She had trouble finding the perfect specimen.

One afternoon my mother and she went grocery shopping, and when they returned, Julie was carrying what she called *a really nice carcass* they'd spotted on Route 1. She dumped it onto the kitchen counter, sliced it neatly, and slid the raccoon out of its fur. "Skinning an animal is as simple as taking off its jacket—that is, if it had a jacket," she said. She held up the shiny sack of entrails for me to admire. "See? They're encased just like they're in a Glad bag."

The first time that I remember believing in God, I was on the playground in the middle of a downpour in second grade. I say *the middle of* because I was literally sitting in a circle of light with rain falling all around me. When I looked at the sky, I saw a splash of sunlight pouring down between the clouds—on me, no one else. I sat there, feeling glowy, and watched the other children run past, including Phoebe, the mean queen of our class, looking like a drowned rat, her hands over her head as if she could hold off the rain. Mrs. Ramsey, the teacher, stood by the door, yelling "Hurry up! Come inside!" I didn't budge. Hadn't the minister, my father's friend, said just the night before that God is like a bright light washing over you, cleansing your spirit? Now it was happening. I sat on the swing set, gazing up at heaven. My soul, I decided, was taking a bath. Maybe I'd turn out to be the next Moses, Elijah, Noah—someone with a name everyone would learn in Bible school. I imagined a fire catching on a bush nearby, manna falling on the grass. But then the clouds moved. I got soaking wet. At the end of the day, Mrs. Ramsey handed me a note for my parents. "Why did you stay out in a rainstorm?" my father asked that evening, shaking the ice in his cocktail glass. "I thought God chose me," I said, "but then He changed his mind." My mother laughed, food falling from her mouth. But my father nodded, "That sounds like God to me."

"You washed your hands?" my father was always asking me. He watched me dip my fingers in the honey jar, lick, then dip again. "Yep," I said, taking another dip before sliding my hands into my pockets. A fly buzzed down, danced its feet on the rim in the jar, then flew off in sharp-angled turns before landing on the fly strip swinging from the ceiling light. "But you just came up from the barn?" he asked. I pointed at the fly strip. "Did you know male flies have crossed eyes just like me? But not lady flies?" I didn't want to admit that I'd been in the chicken coop, collecting eggs. That I'd hunted for kittens in the hayloft, found the newborns with their eyes sealed shut. I'd fed handfuls of fresh-pulled grass to my heifers and apples to Annabelle, the sick pony—she delicately lifted each one with her big yellow teeth. My father grabbed my wrist and held it up to the light, showing off the greenish slime on my hand where cows had licked me. "It doesn't matter," my mother said, glancing up from stirring the eggs. "Honey is a natural antibiotic. She'll be fine."

The youngest child, I worshiped my sisters. Before I was old enough to go to school, I'd wait by the picture window for them to come home. I begged to be included and played whatever they wanted, even Julie's favorite game, which, one winter, was pretending we were dead. She would lie down in a giant cardboard box she called her coffin while I, her ghost, tiptoed around her on sock-feet and hooted like an owl. I asked once if I could be dead, too, but she shook her head. "Only one cadaver is allowed in a coffin," she said. "Don't you know anything?"

When I was sick with the flu for two weeks, she felt sorry for me and let me take a turn in her casket. She even placed a pillow at one end of the box. I felt so happy, lying there, watching the light change in the window, a single cardinal on the tree limb outside, a crimson spot against the white winter sky.

A Good Year to Die

There hadn't been a drop of rain since April when a hot wind blew into town after the dogwood blossom festival and coated the streets in white petals. If you had been riding in a plane and just happened to look down, you might have thought it was snow, but in a few days all the petals turned brown and smelled like rotten apricots. I'd never smelled rotten apricots before then, but when I smell them now, I think of that year when I turned twelve, when everything went south, the year I first understood my parents' marriage wasn't like everyone else's, the year the chickens stopped laying, the cows' milk soured before it reached the table, and the corn barely came out of the ground before the earworms and the Japanese beetles moved in, and all their tassels turned to slime. It was a year folks called a good year to die since no one was having any fun being alive. In fact, the local paper had to hire extra staff just to cover the obituaries. Or that's what my father said. My mother said, "The man exaggerates. You can't believe a word he says." My father just sat in the corner chair, rocking, staring into space, the rhythmic squeak-squeak of the screws coming loose, his only response.

That was also the year the minister, the man my mother called *your father's special friend* moved to a new parish in Alabama. After he left, my father looked so sad, his shirts usually crisp, were sweat- stained and rumpled, and his gaze was permanently trained on the horizon as he filled and refilled his whiskey glass. It was then I noticed how age had erased his chin and eyebrows as well as his awareness of which of his children were living at home. He barely saw me when I sat beside him. "Julie? Louisa? Sal?" he asked, trying to remember my name before settling on Rhubarb, the nickname he used for all his children as well as the plumber, the electrician, the farmhands, and the Rottweiler. Only my mother refused to respond to Rhubarb.

"Yes, Dad," I answered. I didn't want him to feel bad. Besides, I liked being anyone else.

By July the heat was so intense, it slipped under everyone's skin and singed their insides, making my parents simmer and fight. "We're just bickering," my mother said, but they never stopped. It was so hot, no one could sleep at night, and no one could stay awake during the day. Even the flies stopped buzzing. The few that took flight fell out of the air and rolled over on their backs, their little legs kicking one last time. It was so hot the crickets started a fire in Joe Milton's alfalfa field, just by rubbing their legs together. Black smoke filled the horizon; you could hear the sirens screaming for days as the fire spread, flaring up minutes after being put out. It was so hot that when my father went down to the garden to water the vegetables in the morning, he found the tomatoes burst open at the seams. He said he didn't have to cook them. They were already fried. You could just stir them into your grits for breakfast. "I don't like cooked tomatoes in my grits," my mother sulked. "You don't know what you're missing," my father said. "I don't miss what you miss," my mother snapped.

Maybe it was the rage flickering between my parents, maybe it was just bad luck, but I took sick the night before my mother and siblings left for our annual vacation in Maine, my fever spiking so high, my father said he needed oven mitts just to touch my forehead. My mother shook her head. "Sick again?" she asked. The next morning, I watched everyone pile into the station wagon. I insisted I felt better, begging, "Please let me come, too," but my mother said she wasn't having me puking all over the airplane. I cried, watching the dust cloud rise when they drove off. My father patted my head and walked me into the house where he poured himself a bourbon and me *a little nip*: whiskey with lemon and three sugar cubes. "Now this is good medicine," he said, handing me the glass. We sat outside, listening to the silence after everyone had gone. "Isn't this grand?" my father asked. I nodded. It *was* kinda nice, sipping whiskey side by side, feeling our liquor-love burn a hole inside my gut.

After we sat on the lawn for a spell, sipping drinks and looking at each other, noting, *it's just you and me now*, I felt something like relief. Or grace. Maybe it was just the temperature dropping, a cool breeze blowing in, the trees dancing and throwing their shadows all over the ground, but my father grew taller right then, right in front of my eyes. Like the bones fit back into his body. Caleb, the new farmhand walked up from the barn, a stalk of meadow grass in his teeth. "Looks like ya'll be by your lonesome now," he grinned and ran his fingers through his long hair that curled up above his forehead and down his back in a yellow ponytail. That was the year even the farm men started growing their hair long. My father had a thing for hair. So did I. We stared at him, the two of us combing his hair with our eyes.

5:00 was the cocktail hour. My father and I would sit outside, he in his pale summer suit and tie after a day at the office, and I in a flowered shirt and shorts, leaning my chin on my freckled knees, watching bats divebomb mosquitoes. *Lots of sugar,* I'd call out as my father poured our drinks, stirring the amber liquid with his finger. He said developing a taste for liquor is an important social skill, something important to have for the future, sort of like an appreciation of classical music. Sometimes he'd put *Peter and the Wolf* on the stereo (my favorite music since I was a child) and open the window so we could listen to the story along with the songs of the cicadas and katydids. I'd sit back, sucking hard on my straw every time the French horn began, and Peter left the garden gate open. I watched the darkness bleed into the sky as the wolf slunk behind the trees.

One weekend, my father's friend, the minister, came back to town to gather a few last things and visited for what he called evening drinks, arriving when I was supposed to be asleep. I sat by my window watching the men on the terrace, listening to their chatter, soft as the shadows sinking into the folds of my father's suit, the clink of ice in their drinks. The minister drank Scotch on the rocks. My father, Whiskey Tonic. The first night the minister stayed for an hour, the next, over two hours. The night after that, I lost track. I watched the darkness rise, their faces lit by the soft glow of the porch lights, moths fluttering overhead. My father peeled off his coat and unbuttoned his shirt, and the minister removed his collar before reaching for my father's hand. I wanted to shout or bang on my window, but instead I stayed silent and let them remain, as if on the inside of the evening with the scent of rain and heat lightning. They were staring so hard at one a other, listening so closely, I knew they didn't notice the change of rhythm, the insects rubbing their wings together, or the sudden rise in temperature and barometric pressure, the outbreak of songs from tree frogs as the clouds piled higher and higher in the sky and closed over the rooftops, and thunder began. First a rumble. Then a flash of lightning. Then a loud bang before the downpour began. In the morning it would be clear again. The minister gone, my father humming, frying the eggs and bacon. I would know. Nothing happened. Not even when my mother was out of town.

I woke late one morning after my father left for work and noticed a rash like a thousand pinpricks spread over my hands and feet. I called my mother in Maine who assured me it was just chiggers. Or maybe hives or a hay rash. Nothing to worry about. Feeling a little dizzy, I headed on down to the cowbarn, past the pigsty and my father's beehives, and hauled a few buckets of grain to the calves before I looked out across the pastures and watched the grass and trees begin to spin in slow circles as if they were riding on a lazy Susan. Before I knew it, the earth rose up to my face. I remember it as if it were happening to someone else—the sound of my head hitting a rock like a ripe cantaloupe smacking something hard, little white seeds spilling onto the grass. Then I went dark. When I woke and touched my head, it was wrapped in gauze. Charles, the farmhand on parole, had driven me to the ER, even though he didn't have a license. He stood by when the doctor diagnosed me with Rocky Mountain Spotted Fever, said I needed to stay quiet and do nothing for a spell; the disease could be life-threatening. I could have died as quick as a light being shut off.

After my visit to the ER, the farmhands complained about me hanging around the barn. They said they couldn't be held responsible if I fell again. My father hired Charlene West (the governess, he called her) to look after me. "I'm twelve years old—way too old for a babysitter," I sulked and refused to come downstairs when she arrived. But as soon as I laid eyes on Charlene, I was smitten. At eighteen Charlene could have risen out of the pages of the Art History book we kept on our coffee table. She was Botticelli's Venus with her long red hair and creamy skin as soft and pale as bread dough. I wanted to press my hands into her flesh and see if I left fingerprints. "You're so white," I said, gazing at her pillowy thighs that squeezed against the hem of her hotpants. "My mama's a beautician," she smiled. "I work in her shop, sorting perm rods, sweeping hair from the floors, giving manicures and makeup-touchups for customers. I help with the hair dyes, too. I change my own hair color every season." I pictured her living in a glass room like a terrarium without a drop of rain or a strand of sunlight creeping in. Nothing changed in there except the color of Charlene's hair.

Charlene and I spent our days on the carpet in front of the box fan flipping through the fashion magazines she brought from the salon. Sometimes she'd lie on her belly, her breasts swaying in twin hammocks from her skimpy top as she chose which models she liked best and which didn't belong on those glossy pages. "The prettiest," she said, "musta lived in heaven because I never seen real gals as pretty as that." She'd decide who she might want to be if only she could lose a few pounds. Farrah Fawcett and Twiggy were her top picks. "But you're prettier than Farrah," I said, and "Twiggy's too skinny. I like your body best." She lowered her eyes, blew out a blast of bubble gum-scented breath and blushed pink as a sunset, heat radiating from her skin.

"I feel sick," I said one afternoon, doubling over in pain. The next day I woke with blood smears on my underpants and sheets. Charlene drove me into town, chatting the whole time. "Imagine, a little thang like you—a lady," she said as she blew a large bubble with her gum and let it splat across her cheeks and chin. At *Rose's Drug and Gifts*, she purchased me two new pairs of underwear, silky and pink—said I needed pretty undergarments now that I was a woman, a box of industrial strength menstrual pads, and Midol. At home she demonstrated how to clip a pad onto a white belt so that it hung beneath my legs like a sling. I managed to belt myself in, and she clapped her hands as if I'd performed a circus act. I was glad it was her and not my dad. But sitting on a menstrual pad was liking sitting on a banana, slipping from one butt cheek to the next. "How do I balance?" I asked. "You'll get used to it," she said. "It's like my mama says: once you turn into a lady, your body ain't your friend no more."

"Now you're a lady let's make you look like one," Charlene said after the Midol kicked in. She washed my hair in the kitchen sink, found my mother's curlers and styling lotion and gave me a set. I sat under the bonnet hairdryer for an hour, my face glowing in the heat. When it was finally dry, she unpinned the rollers, loosened the curls with her fingers, and told me to shake my head before hosing me down with Aqua Net. My hair felt like cotton candy. "Now look at you," she sighed, tugging the curls that boinged around my face. "We just need to add a final touch." She reached into her purse, fished her lipstick out, and knelt before me, twisting open the golden tube and gliding the crimson stick over my lips. "I like it," I said, staring into the mirror. She stepped back, her long red hair swaying like a curtain between us. "Me too," she smiled and took my hand in her moist fingers. "Now our mouths match."

On Charlene's last day, the only day we wandered around the farm, we sunbathed by the pond where farmhands might have seen us. Her red hair was fading, and I traced a line of inky black roots at the top of her scalp. "I'll be blond next, like Brigitte Bardot," she giggled before stripping off her bra and panties. "I don't know about you, but I'm going in!" I stared at her breasts, milk-white with little black hairs around the nipples—like jimmies on vanilla ice cream cones. *Did she see me looking?* I glanced away. That night I dreamt of lifting her hair from her neck, feeling it run through my hands like a silky red waterfall. When I woke and flicked on the light, a solitary bee from my father's hives flew through a hole in the screen and circled the lamp, helpless to resist the forty-watt bulb. *Is this how it starts?* I wondered, remembering how my mother said that men have desires, not women—unless they're nymphomaniacs. *What if I'm one of them? Or worse?* I worried. *What if I like women AND men?*

It was the day after Labor Day, the last day of that summer with just my dad, when he had to take me to the ER again. "Is it menstrual cramps?" the doctor asked after assuring my father that he could stay in the waiting room. I had a fever, nausea, and was so dizzy, I had trouble walking in a straight line. "You'd be surprised how a simple period can do you in," he added. Outside it was raining. I could hear the rhythmic drumming on the roof. I wished Charlene were with me, or my sisters or mother. The doctor, a heavyset man with skin the color of honey, felt my forehead and poked my belly and neck. The fluorescent lights hummed overhead. I was cold, my teeth chattering; my tennis shoes were soaking wet. There were moles on the doctor's neck—I counted them, *one, two, three,* his wine-scented breath, sweet and hot on my face. "It's okay," he said in a foreign accent—it sounded like *saké*. He lifted my hospital gown; the tissue paper floated to the ground. *Saké,* he said again and parted my legs, pressing his gloved hand between my thighs. I sucked in like a hooked fish, opening and closing my mouth, no sound or breath coming out. Long after I felt the stab of his fingers like a hot knife.

The Shadow of a Bird

There is a place you can land by birth or bad luck—another country without sunrise or sunset, without dreams or cigarettes or pets, where only a few can cross over to see you. They hope they can bring you back—of course they don't know. Or they hope they will never visit you again—at least not there. No one wants to see you like that.

You don't tell them how you aged one hundred years in a single night when you tried to give up your story, a tale with no heart, a house full of empty rooms, windows swollen shut, the scent of lemon Endust and loneliness, a cross-eyed girl you never liked, a mind you lost her inside.

How afterwards, your soul rose—a limp balloon, shaking its gray head as it drifted loose. For months, it could not reach you. Or you, it. Though it wished you things: hope, a song, a memory of a doll you slept with as a child before you plucked out its eyes and made its face into a soft, smooth pillow.

The year my body no longer fit, walking felt like swimming in winter clothes. Everything stuck to me: chewing gum, spit, toothpicks, nightmares, men's hands. How I envied the girls at the local swimming hole who lit cigarettes, blew smoke in each other's faces, giggled and dared each other to strip and dive from cliffs. "Jump!" the prettiest called out. One by one, they opened their bare arms and rose on tiptoes, filling the horizon with their winter-white breasts and hips and limbs. What I would have done to join them. But it was my job to breathe in so they could exhale, to shrink so they could ascend, to be the watcher, the witness, the shadow they cast onto the ground.

I was born with a death wish that hovered like a bird on the windowsill of my childhood. Where it flew in from or why, I never knew. "Maybe it's a gene," my mother said. "Maybe it was caused by all the eye surgeries," my doctor suggested. "It's just a consequence of parental neglect," a therapist asserted. "You were abandoned so often, you abandoned yourself." "Therapists always blame the parents," my father said. My mother, a fan of the famous *L'Enfant Sauvage*, wanted us to grow up wild. She bragged that we were farm children, raised by the animals, the wind, the stars, the rain. Sometimes I'd think, I *like being alone. I don't need anyone else.* I wandered down the dirt road and lay beneath the peach trees, smoked my brother's dope, let the shadows crawl over my arms and legs as my dreams turned to ashes and blew away.

My parents are the best, I wrote in my high school journal with my favorite leaky fountain pen, blue blops smearing the letters: *They're so much better than the other parents who are always telling their girls what to do and wear and how and when, taking their photographs, dressing them up like poodles, clapping whenever they sing or dance or count to ten. Me, I can just be who I am.*

Reading those words, I realize I was quoting my mother who always compared women to poodles. Once, years later, when I was complaining about my parents, she said, "Admittedly your father had his bouts of ill temper. Or madness, as you call it. But they never lasted. Just think how much you have to thank us for. How else would you have learned to love birds, cows, horses, whiskey, Greek myths, and what I prefer to call *artistic men?*"

"Set the saltshaker down! Careful now. Don't spill a grain," my father instructed. He practiced every superstition including some I suspect he made up. So I did, too. If I spilled salt, I tossed a few grains right hand over left shoulder, not the other way around. "No, not that right hand, you nitwit," my father said. I was five, six, seven; I was ten, eleven, twelve . . . I forgot things no matter how old I was. I hung the horseshoe upside down, let the luck leak out. I let the cat out the bag. I let the beagle in the henhouse—he shot between my legs. I let the bird in the open window when we were cleaning the glass. "Look, it's flying all over the place. Feathers everywhere," my father said. "That's a bad omen, I'll tell you what. First sickness then death."

I ducked under the table when my father was mad, ducked and held my breath as if we were driving under a bridge or through a tunnel or past a graveyard. I turned red, then blue—I wanted to breathe so bad, but if I did, the wrong dead (not one of my loved ones like my late nanny, grandparents, or Aunt Ada) might slip in and steal my dreams or finger my dress—or that's what my father said. I squeezed a rabbit's foot in my left hand—a left rabbit's foot in my left hand because that's how the magic worked. Then I chanted *amen, amen, amen.*

The dead, according to my father, are watching you all the time, listening in on your thoughts and conversations. They bristle when you speak ill of them, glow when you pray for them and miss them. If you ask them questions, they answer in your dreams. They trade places with you every twenty minutes, slipping inside your skin and quickly out again. If you are in a crowded room, and the room falls silent, the dead are trading places with the living. That's the origin of the term, dead silence. If you look closely, you can see them as they leave, fading away like strands of moonlight in the middle of the day.

I don't know when my habit of repeating things began: repeating thoughts, words, dialogs, playing them back in my head, wishing I could correct them. In high school I didn't talk much—instead I silently rehearsed what I wished to say. I became quiet, thinking and rethinking. The problem grew worse with writing—my typed pages, heavy with white-out. (This was before computers.) When I composed an essay, I revised it page by page, paragraph by paragraph, sentence by sentence, word by word. Sometimes, a homework assignment took days, a paragraph, hours, and the sentences with all those words, so many words to choose from, so many meanings, so much distance opening up between what I thought and what I wrote on the page. Words, I imagined were like stones in a river, the mind rushing overhead, trying to reach and grab the prettiest, the shiniest, the luckiest, the best before the moment passed. "You write like a poet," my high school English teacher said. "Consider it a gift." *A gift*, I wondered, *or a sign of mental illness?*

It was a Sunday afternoon in my junior year of high school when I first realized I needed help. My father must have known as well. I was standing in the bathroom when suddenly, as if on a whim, I took his straight razor and ran it up and down the soft belly flesh of my forearm. *I can do this*, I thought. I stood there, staring at the bright red blood against the white sink when my father walked in. He looked at the blood, the razor, me. Neither of us said a word. Then he turned and left, closing the door behind him.

"May I see a therapist?" I asked my mother. "Of course not. Psychiatrists are not real doctors," she snapped. I secretly made an appointment with Dr. Wilkes, the only woman therapist in town, biking to her office on a Wednesday afternoon in October—a homey office in a yellow clapboard house near the university. For exactly fifty minutes, I talked quickly, trying not to correct myself. Dr. Wilkes said nothing, her silence, a static hum in my head. Before I left, I handed her my journal, said I hoped it would help with my diagnosis. I paid her with my clothing allowance.

Days later, my father invited my high school principal to the house for cocktails. After the two men had been talking for a while, I was invited to join them. "We've decided you don't need a therapist," my father announced as I entered the room. He handed me my journal and the wad of bills I had paid to Dr. Wilkes. "You're just an ordinary adolescent. I should know—you're my last teenager."

On weekend nights in high school, I lay on my bed, staring out the window. A lunar moth pressed its pale green wings against the panes. I wished I had the nerve to say *yes* to the boy who kept asking me to the movies. Or the energy to read a novel. Sometimes, I drifted downstairs to the living room where my father was reading the paper. "You don't look too happy," he'd say before pouring me a bourbon. We sat on the couch, sipping in silence, waiting for the evening to dissolve and soften around the edges—for that lit feeling I still call my daddy glow.

On weekend nights in college, I sat at my desk in my hot room where the radiator blazed, heat rising despite the winter air rushing in the open windows. I typed and retyped essays until the pages spilled onto the floor beside me. I rarely slept. Even when I lay down to rest, I stared into space, watching whole paragraphs revise themselves in my head. I would rise, make a cup of coffee or swallow a NoDoz, and start writing again. "Just turn in what you have," a college counselor advised. "But I'm not finished," I said.

I can't go on like this, I thought. One night I fell asleep at my desk and dreamt I was in a greenhouse, light filtering through the drippy panes, plants climbing the walls, the wet air drenching my hair. Someone was stroking my head. "You can rest now," a voice said. When I looked up, I saw Winter Grandmother as a woman my age—young and soft, her hair billowing above her head like smoke. How pretty she looked in a white dress. "Am I dead like you?" I asked. She pressed my hand and cool light traveled up my arm. "Not yet," she said, adding, "I was suicidal once, too." I woke with the feeling of her touch lingering on my wrist.

"There are things we don't talk about," my father said, but I never knew which "things" he meant. Even after my suicide attempt, my father wanted to control my story. If anyone asked why I was home from college, he told me to say I was just taking a break. "The less you talk, the better off we will all be," he advised. "The way I see it—there are things this world doesn't need to know. After all, everyone has dark moments—times when they see night in the middle of the afternoon."

"But what if you see night all the time?" I asked.

After my parents picked me up from a hospital near Bryn Mawr College and drove me home to the farm, I lay in my bed for days, weeks, or was it months? My father called me Sleeping Beauty. Sometimes he brought me peanut butter sandwiches and a ginger ale on a silver tray and left them on my bedside table. But my mother didn't want to see me. She was afraid of mental illness. How could I be sick *like that?* she whispered. And as a Bryn Mawr graduate, she was furious. "How dare you embarrass me?"

"How many bottles of aspirin did you consume?" she demanded on the rare day she came to my room, glaring down at me as I lay in bed, eyes pressed shut. "And how many pills were in each bottle?" She always counted things. Numbers, she once told me when I was struggling with math, explain everything. I didn't have the energy to respond. There was a fog in my head, and I couldn't assemble the right words. All my thoughts were scrambled like an ancient TV screen with no antennae.

If I wasn't asleep, I was daydreaming about bridges to jump from, trains to step in front of, and pills of all shapes and colors, wondering which ones and how many equals an overdose. The ER doctor in Bryn Mawr had lifted my hospital gown and sighed. "Such a pretty body—it would be a shame to kill it just yet. But if you're serious, try Tylenol next—it usually does the trick." His name was Derrick. I remember that, and his clammy hand on my breasts and a fly buzzing around the Pepsi by my bed. I thought of Emily Dickinson, "I heard a fly buzz when I died."

"Did Grandma ever try to kill herself?" I asked my mother once. I wanted to trace the lineage of the death wish. My cousin Bobby and I, maybe Grandma—were we the only ones? And why did so many writers kill themselves? I had planned to major in English, and I could list the famous literary suicides—Ernest Hemingway shot himself in the head in his study; John Berryman jumped from The Washington Avenue Bridge in Minneapolis; Hart Crane threw himself from the steamship SS *Orizaba*; Anne Sexton locked herself in a car with the engine running, and then there was Sylvia Plath who made suicide into an art. I read everything she wrote, and admired and envied her—I wondered if I were a talented poet, as manic and as pretty as she was, would I become eternally famous, too?

Virginia Woolf was the writer I worshiped, Virginia with the name of my home state, Virginia of the waves with a room of her own and a lighthouse, Virginia who drowned with a pocketful of stones. She reminded me of the time I almost drowned off the coast of South Carolina while my parents were walking the beach. I remember inhaling water, trying to call for help, and being swept further and further away. How alone I felt with the sun, the ocean, the endless blue sky. I imagined the world, as if I were already on the other side, looking back through a one-way mirror.

I read and reread the note Virginia Woolf left her husband. "Dearest, I feel certain that I am going mad again. I feel I can't go through another of these terrible times. And I shan't recover this time. I hear voices, and I can't concentrate. So I am doing what seems the best thing to do." I reread the words, *the best thing to do.* What is the best thing to do when you're going mad? I thought of how my mother always said, "Don't tell anyone if you're hearing voices. And don't ever mention the visions of death you had as a child." I kept hearing Virginia's voice repeating, "Do the best thing."

"Do you think I should see a doctor?" I asked my parents on a rare night when they both came to check on me in my room. My mouth tasted like a swamp. Moss was beginning to grow on my back and legs. My father shook his head. He said our town was too small. There were no doctors he would allow me to see. "Time heals everything," my mother added blithely. "Just get some rest. Maybe you'll feel better in the morning." When she closed the door behind them, I felt so cold, like that ache in winter when you forgot to wear a coat, and all the blood has left your feet and hands. Right before the numbness sets in.

I don't know how or when I left the bed in that foggy room in my childhood home in Charlottesville, Virginia. I have no memory of packing my bags, boarding an airplane, or flying to Seattle, or moving in with my sister, Sal, who was studying at the University of Washington. I don't remember living in Seattle. Did it rain? It must have rained. Was it cold? I think so. Did I continue to sleep all day there?

I saw a psychiatrist several days a week, but I don't remember him. I hear he was a young doctor, doing research for his PhD on endorphins. He wrote a note: *You must exercise every day. No excuses.* Did I run? Swim? I don't know. Just as I don't remember what he or his office looked like, if he was tall or brawny or blond or bearded, or if I sat up facing him or lay down as I've always wanted to do during therapy, stretching out on my back and confessing to the ceiling.

I do remember driving around the city in my sister's green Volvo, sucking on carob pods, which I'd never eaten before. I remember they tasted of dirt and chocolate and mold, and I sucked them until they dissolved into a fibrous mush. I remember eating the stale taffy my sister left under the car seat, whole bags of candy that stuck to my teeth and gave me cavities. I chewed the skin from around my fingertips until all ten fingers bled, and I kept chewing, bleeding, the taste of iron on my tongue. I remember one night my sister handed me a joint, and I smoked it quickly, sucking in hard. The marijuana filled my head with a dense murky cloud. "You will feel better soon. I know it," my sister said.

"How do you know?" I asked. "I just know," she said. "Don't you?" "Yes," I lied. She was so determined, so kind, I couldn't say no. *Lying*, I thought, *is my true gift.*

And I remember waking one morning in Seattle to sunlight flooding my room. A city of rain was suddenly neon, bathed in light. Yes, bathed. Light spilled down my walls, puddled on the floor. *This can't be,* I thought. *What happened? Did I move to Santa Fe?* I missed my clouds. Words like *bliss* and *glory* and even *lo and behold* filled my mind as an alien joy swept through my veins like an electric current. I didn't like it—it wasn't me, this light, this happiness, this blazing blue sky.

It can't last, I thought when I woke, day after day, feeling uncannily happy. *Surely, it will go away. It's just the light that follows the darkness that follows the light. Soon I will be myself—dark and rainy and neurotic again.*

What do I do with all this joy inside me? I stared in the mirror. *Who the hell are you?* I asked. That's when the past rushed back in. Whole pages of my life fluttered around me. I tried to catch them with my pen. I couldn't write fast enough.

"I feel so good, I'm scared!" I told my sister when I came downstairs after hours of writing at my desk. She lit up a joint to celebrate.

"I'm bipolar, right?" I asked a therapist a few years later. "Shouldn't I cycle downhill again? And again?"

"A diagnosis," he answered, "is not a life sentence."

On the same day I woke up from depression, a boyfriend from high school wrote me a letter about a tiny sedentary insect, as ugly and homely as a moth. Named the St. Francis's Satyr, it flew off the extinction list onto Fort Bragg's artillery range where it thrives amidst natural disturbances: fire, flooding, and the destruction of its habitat. He sent me a photograph of the butterfly, which I kept in a book for years. "Like you, she's a survivor," he scribbled on the back. I didn't know I had a boyfriend in high school. In subsequent letters, he called me his little brown butterfly. "Really?" I asked. Other friends wrote me, too. I felt them like wings, opening and closing on my back.

Whiskey on the rocks, my father's evening drink. Mine, whiskey sours: whiskey, lemon, sugar. "More sugar," I'd say as my father poured and stirred it in with his finger. My first drink, I was four. "Just a small glass," my father said as my mother looked on. I pressed the cold tumbler against my forehead and held it up to see the light coming through the liquid, golden like the meadow in August, like Triscuits, like the halo in paintings of Christ. I tilted my head back and sipped. It was love at first taste: the sweetness, the burn, the lightness inside my head.

My first joint, I was twelve. I remember it was a balmy Friday after school. I was climbing down the ladder from the hayloft when I saw Charles, the farmhand, leaning against the fence, a doobie between his oil-stained fingers. "Want a toke?" he asked. He showed me how to inhale and hold my breath. I coughed until tears rolled down my cheeks. "That's okay, try again," he laughed. Afterwards, I lay back in the meadow, feeling grasshoppers cling to my legs with their Velcro claws. "Grasshoppers," I told them, "you are my best friends."

I know what you're thinking—I must be an addict. Whiskey, even just seeing a bottle on the shelf, makes me think of my father, everything I loved about the man. Marijuana, a whiff of the putrid smell on a street corner, reminds me of the farmhands and my sister Sal and teenage friends and late-night laughter. But I haven't drunk whiskey or smoked a joint since my twenties.

Endorphins are my fix now. *Run, swim, bike!* the therapist wrote on a prescription pad. And I do. Like a rat on a wheel. In my mind, I still see the shadow of a bird circling overhead.

About the Author

Nin Andrews is the author of the six chapbooks and ten full-length poetry collections including *The Last Orgasm* (2020), *Miss August* (2017), and *Why God is a Woman* (2015). She is the recipient of two Ohio individual artists grants, the Pearl Chapbook prize, The Wick Chapbook Prize, and the Gerald Cable Award. Her book, *Southern Comfort*, was a finalist for the Forward Prize for Poetry 2010, and her collection, *Why God is a Woman* won the Ohiona Prize for Poetry in 2016. Her work has been featured in numerous journals and anthologies including *Ploughshares, Agni, The Paris Review*, four editions of *Best American Poetry, Great American Prose Poems from Poe to the Present*, and *The Best American Erotic Poems*. Her poetry has been translated into Turkish, performed in Prague and anthologized in England, Australia, and Mongolia. She is also the editor of a book of translations of the Belgian writer, Henri Michaux.

Books From Etruscan Press

Zarathustra Must Die | Dorian Alexander
The Disappearance of Seth | Kazim Ali
The Last Orgasm | Nin Andrews
Drift Ice | Jennifer Atkinson
Crow Man | Tom Bailey
Coronology | Claire Bateman
Viscera | Felice Belle
Reading the Signs and other itinerant essays | Stephen Benz
Topographies | Stephen Benz
What We Ask of Flesh | Remica L. Bingham
The Greatest Jewish-American Lover in Hungarian History | Michael Blumenthal
No Hurry | Michael Blumenthal
Choir of the Wells | Bruce Bond
Cinder | Bruce Bond
The Other Sky | Bruce Bond and Aron Wiesenfeld
Peal | Bruce Bond
Scar | Bruce Bond
Until We Talk | Darrell Bourque and Bill Gingles
Big Time | Rus Bradburd
Poems and Their Making: A Conversation | Moderated by Philip Brady
Crave: Sojourn of a Hungry Soul | Laurie Jean Cannady
Toucans in the Arctic | Scott Coffel
Sixteen | Auguste Corteau
Don't Mind Me | Brian Coughlan
Wattle & daub | Brian Coughlan
Body of a Dancer | Renée E. D'Aoust
Generations: Lullaby with Incendiary Device, The Nazi Patrol, and How It Is That We | Dante Di Stefano, William Heyen, and H. L. Hix
Ill Angels | Dante Di Stefano

Aard-vark to Axolotl: Pictures From my Grandfather's Dictionary | Karen Donovan
Trio: Planet Parable, Run: A Verse-History of Victoria Woodhull, and Endless Body | Karen Donovan, Diane Raptosh, and Daneen Wardrop
Scything Grace | Sean Thomas Dougherty
Areas of Fog | Will Dowd
Romer | Robert Eastwood
Wait for God to Notice | Sari Fordham
Bon Courage: Essays on Inheritance, Citizenship, and a Creative Life | Ru Freeman
Surrendering Oz | Bonnie Friedman
Funeral Playlist | Sarah Gorham
Nahoonkara | Peter Grandbois
Triptych: The Three-Legged World, In Time, and Orpheus & Echo | Peter Grandbois, James McCorkle, and Robert Miltner
The Candle: Poems of Our 20th Century Holocausts | William Heyen
The Confessions of Doc Williams & Other Poems | William Heyen
The Football Corporations | William Heyen
A Poetics of Hiroshima | William Heyen
September 11, 2001: American Writers Respond | Edited by William Heyen
Shoah Train | William Heyen
American Anger: An Evidentiary | H. L. Hix
As Easy As Lying | H. L. Hix
As Much As, If Not More Than | H. L. Hix
Chromatic | H. L. Hix
Demonstrategy: Poetry, For and Against | H. L. Hix
First Fire, Then Birds | H. L. Hix
God Bless | H. L. Hix
I'm Here to Learn to Dream in Your Language | H. L. Hix
Incident Light | H. L. Hix
Legible Heavens | H. L. Hix

Lines of Inquiry | H. L. Hix
Rain Inscription | H. L. Hix
Shadows of Houses | H. L. Hix
Wild and Whirling Words: A Poetic Conversation | Moderated by H. L. Hix
All the Difference | Patricia Horvath
Art Into Life | Frederick R. Karl
Free Concert: New and Selected Poems | Milton Kessler
Who's Afraid of Helen of Troy: An Essay on Love | David Lazar
Black Metamorphoses | Shanta Lee
Mailer's Last Days: New and Selected Remembrances of a Life in Literature | J. Michael Lennon
Parallel Lives | Michael Lind
The Burning House | Paul Lisicky
Museum of Stones | Lynn Lurie
Quick Kills | Lynn Lurie
Synergos | Roberto Manzano
The Gambler's Nephew | Jack Matthews
American Mother | Colum McCann with Diane Foley
The Subtle Bodies | James McCorkle
An Archaeology of Yearning | Bruce Mills
Arcadia Road: A Trilogy | Thorpe Moeckel
Venison | Thorpe Moeckel
So Late, So Soon | Carol Moldaw
The Widening | Carol Moldaw
Clay and Star: Selected Poems of Liliana Ursu | Translated by Mihaela Moscaliuc
Cannot Stay: Essays on Travel | Kevin Oderman
White Vespa | Kevin Oderman
Also Dark | Angelique Palmer
Fates: The Medea Notebooks, Starfish Wash-Up, and overflow of an unknown self | Ann Pedone, Katherine Soniat, and D. M. Spitzer
The Dog Looks Happy Upside Down | Meg Pokrass
Mr. Either/Or | Aaron Poochigian
Mr. Either/Or: All the Rage | Aaron Poochigian
The Shyster's Daughter | Paula Priamos

Help Wanted: Female | Sara Pritchard
American Amnesiac | Diane Raptosh
Dear Z: The Zygote Epistles | Diane Raptosh
Human Directional | Diane Raptosh
I Eric America | Diane Raptosh
50 *Miles* | Sheryl St. Germain
Saint Joe's Passion | J.D. Schraffenberger
Lies Will Take You Somewhere | Sheila Schwartz
Fast Animal | Tim Seibles
One Turn Around the Sun | Tim Seibles
Voodoo Libretto: New and Selected Poems | Tim Seibles
Rough Ground | Alix Anne Shaw
A Heaven Wrought of Iron: Poems From the Odyssey | D. M. Spitzer
American Fugue | Alexis Stamatis
Variations in the Key of K | Alex Stein
The Casanova Chronicles | Myrna Stone
Luz Bones | Myrna Stone
In the Cemetery of the Orange Trees | Jeff Talarigo
The White Horse: A Colombian Journey | Diane Thiel
The Arsonist's Song Has Nothing to Do With Fire | Allison Titus
Bestiality of the Involved | Spring Ulmer
The Waw | Jacqueline Gay Walley
Silk Road | Daneen Wardrop
Sinnerman | Michael Waters
The Fugitive Self | John Wheatcroft
YOU. | Joseph P. Wood
Leaves Borrowed from Human Flesh | Abigail Ardelle Zammit

Etruscan Press Is Proud of Support Received From

Wilkes University

Ohio Arts Council

The Stephen & Jeryl Oristaglio Foundation

Community of Literary Magazines and Presses

National Endowment for the Arts

Drs. Barbara Brothers & Gratia Murphy Endowment

Founded in 2001 with a generous grant from the Oristaglio Foundation, Etruscan Press is a nonprofit cooperative of poets and writers working to produce and promote books that nurture the dialogue among genres, achieve a distinctive voice, and reshape the literary and cultural histories of which we are a part.

Etruscan press
www.etruscanpress.org

Etruscan Press books may be ordered from
Consortium Book Sales and Distribution
800.283.3572
www.cbsd.com

Etruscan Press is a 501(c)(3) nonprofit organization.
Contributions to Etruscan Press are tax deductible
as allowed under applicable law.
For more information, a prospectus,
or to order one of our titles,
contact us at books@etruscanpress.org.

www.ingramcontent.com/pod-product-compliance
Lightning Source LLC
Jackson TN
JSHW081640090226
97521JS00001B/1
* 9 7 9 8 9 8 8 1 9 8 5 9 8 *